# Wipe Out All Student Loan Debt—Now!

### Unique solutions to the $1.8 Trillion debt accumulation

The President in simple terms has netted out the student debt crisis from both a student and parent perspective: "They go, and they work, and they take loans, and they're borrowed up, and they can't breathe, and they get through college and the worst thing is, they go through that whole process and they don't have any job." Trump has it right, and worse than that, when the US system hurts them, our best and brightest lose hope.

Many have excoriated the Obama Administration and government and coffee-breath professors who teach nothing, for making it worse for college graduates. They all make money on the student loan program. Trump says: "You know the one program that the U.S. makes a whole lot of money with is student loans, and that's maybe the one program they shouldn't be making money with… "So, we're going to have to start a program," he said. "We're going to do something very big with loans because you have to get these people going. They really feel down and out."

Donald J. Trump is right. Yet he is the only president who has even talked about solving America's problem with rip-off loan sharks and a government that makes big money off the backs of student borrowers. Ironically, the man willing to help is hated by the very young Americans he speaks about helping.

College graduates and those former students not fortunate enough to complete their degrees need all the help they can get to claw their way out of their college debt. Your author as a professor and as a father understands student debt. He feels and has intellectually analyzed the plight and the pain felt by today's millennials. Besides recommending a total forgiveness and a do-again, this book also examines other ways to solve the problem including refinancing, extending, and providing better payment plans as well as getting universities to put some skin in the game.

This book addresses the massive $1.45 Trillion student debt already on the books and it presents a boldly unique plan to assure that students with loans have a chance of success with a job of their choice. Isn't it about time? This book tells you how it can be done. You won't be able to put this book down before you know what you can do to help those with student debt be able to afford homes and start families and live the life of a real American and not an indentured servant.

## BRIAN W. KELLY

Copyright 2018 Brian W. Kelly  Editor, Brian P. Kelly
Wipe Out all Student Loan Debt Now!  Author Brian W. Kelly
**Unique solutions to the $1.8 Trillion debt accumulation**

**All rights reserved:** No part of this book may be reproduced or transmitted in any form, or by any means, electronic or mechanical, including photocopying, recording, scanning, faxing, or by any information storage and retrieval system, without permission from the publisher, LETS GO PUBLISH, in writing.

**Disclaimer:** Though judicious care was taken throughout the writing and the publication of this work that the information contained herein is accurate, there is no expressed or implied warranty that all information in this book is 100% correct. Therefore, neither LETS GO PUBLISH, nor the author accepts liability for any use of this work.

**Trademarks:** A number of products and names referenced in this book are trade names and trademarks of their respective companies.

**Referenced Material:** *The information in this book has been obtained through personal and third-party observations, interviews, and copious research. Where unique information has been provided or extracted from other sources, those sources are acknowledged within the text of the book itself or at the end of the chapter in the Sources Section. Thus, there are no formal footnotes nor is there a bibliography section. Any picture that does not have a source was taken from various sites on the Internet with no credit attached. If resource owners would like credit in the next printing, please email publisher.*

**Published by**: LETS GO PUBLISH!
**Publisher:** Brian P. Kelly
**Editor:** Brian P. Kelly
P.O Box 621 Wilkes-Barre, PA   www.letsgopublish.com

Library of Congress Copyright Information Pending
Book Cover Design by Michele Thomas; Editing by Brian P. Kelly

**ISBN Information:** The International Standard Book Number (ISBN) is a unique machine-readable identification number, which marks any book unmistakably. The ISBN is the clear standard in the book industry. 159 countries and territories are officially ISBN members. The Official ISBN For this book is also on the outside cover:   **978-1-947402-23-2**

---

The price for this work is:                              $12.95 USD

10   9   8   7   6   5   4   3   2   1

Release Date:                                         January 2018

# *Dedication*

*I dedicate this book to my wonderful wife Patricia; our three wonderful children Brian, Mike and Katie; and our friendly friends—Ben our very happy dog, who recently became an Angel, and Buddy, our always cheerful cat.*

*Thank You All!*

# Acknowledgments

*I appreciate all the help that I have received in putting this book together as well as all of my other 135 other published books.*

*My printed acknowledgments had become so large that book readers "complained" about going through too many pages to get to page one of the text.*

*And, so to permit me more flexibility, I put my acknowledgment list online, and it continues to grow. Believe it or not, it once cost about a dollar more to print each book.*

*Thank you and God bless you all for your help.*

*Please check out [www.letsgopublish.com](www.letsgopublish.com) to read the latest version of my heartfelt acknowledgments updated for this book. FYI, Wily Ky Eyely loves this book and recommends it to all other 11-year old little Maesters*

*Click the bottom of the Main menu!*

*Thank you all!*

# Preface:

Rarely does a book title explain exactly what a book is about. This book is the exception. Wiping out all student loan debt now will immediately solve the student debt crisis. There is no question about it.

It helps to recall that President Obama increased the National Debt by $9.1 Trillion in just eight years, hoping to assure that illegal aliens had all the resources they needed to take as many American jobs as they could. He just about doubled our debt and has nothing to show. Tell me where the money went?

It is too bad that he did not have the foresight to use $1.3 Trillion of that wasteful largesse to help America. With less than 15% of this reckless spending, the former president could have been a folk hero among many Americans.

He could have and should have spent more wisely and wiped out 100% of the student debt now strangling our young American adults and holding the US economy hostage. Until the student debt crisis is put behind us, the most physically capable and more than likely, the brightest people in America, our recent college graduates between the ages of twenty and forty, have been taken out of the game.

They will not be in a position to start a business, buy a home, new appliances, a new car, or begin a family. I am talking about 45 million student loan borrowers—seventy percent of all college students / graduates. At a time that we needed Obama's leadership the most, right after the sub-prime mortgage crisis when the economy was at a standstill, how could the former president have missed the opportunity to reinvigorate the economy by freeing 45 million young people from debtor's prison.

The former president had the opportunity to reinsert forty-five million Americans with a propensity to spend money into the economy and he did not choose to act. He chose not to free them from the shackles of repaying a massive and unfair student debt load that will keep them out of the economy for years and years to come.

This book tells Congress and the new president how to solve the crisis and it tells American that nothing happens without a vigilant population. That means we must hold our government and our politicians accountable for solving this crisis that affects almost every family in America.

More and more Americans, even those of us who have paid off all of our student debt are looking at today's student loan dilemma with a different look. The groundswell of concern for removing so many potentially productive Americans from the economy at one time is at an all-time high with more Americans asking Washington to forgive this debt so that young Americans can engage and so that the economy can be jump-started to make all Americans successful.

Yung Americans are literally choking on their student debt. It has their lives stopped and each year that it not solved is another day in a veritable debtor's prison. It is so bad that 50% in a recent survey would be willing to give up their most fundamental freedom to be able to lead a normal life.

A survey from Credible, conducted through Pollfish, hits the seriousness of the situation right on the head. It is understandable that young Americans would want a chance in life by having their debt removed. But it was surprising to many what they would be willing to do to be free of those loans. The most popular answer the 500 respondents between the ages of 18 and 34 chose for what they would be desperate enough to sacrifice was *"suffrage."* Yes, half surveyed said they would give up the ability to vote in the next two presidential elections to be able to move their lives forward.

It is not just those who would be set free who feel forgiving student debt is an idea whose time has come. More Americans believe that the US should forgive all federal student debt than feel that the recipients should pay their loans back. The results to many of the survey conducted by MoneyTips.com were shocking. Nearly 42% agreed with the statement, "I believe President Trump's Department of Education should forgive all federal student debt to help the economy."

Less than 37% disagreed, while the remaining 21% neither agreed nor disagreed. Even those who for years were pressuring Congress to do the right thing were taken back. For example, Brandon Yahn, founder of "studentloanguy.com said: "It is surprising that the majority of the US population supports this measure…Perhaps this student debt burden has spread more across all generations, and popular sentiment is turning the corner as it relates to student debt."

When asked further about the positive impact on the economy and the impact of future student's ability to attend college in the future, most believe that this is a one and done. There should never be another forgiveness. And, so the consensus is that there needs to be a fool-proof solution for new student debt so that new high school aspirants to college do not sign up for debt when they do not need to do so.

There are a number of notions in this book besides wiping out all of the $1.45 Trillion. This book discusses most if not all of the theories about how this happened and how it can be made to never happen again. Additionally, it discusses a number of student resources and a few tricks that are both honest and long overdue.

Why did Brian W. Kelly write this book?

Brian W. Kelly wrote this book because he cares about college graduates being able to move on with their lives. I am publishing this book because I care. This book identifies the most notable and most serious flaws in student tuition financing. It then solves them by prescribing a number of Kelly-unique solutions to help get the program back on track.

I hope you enjoy this book and I that it inspires you to take the individual actions necessary to help the government of the US stand firm against any attacks on democracy from outside or from within this great country. A great start of course is to stop the government gouging of young Americans, who are plagued with student debt. Instead government should be a helpful tool in solving this deep moral dilemma for our country.

I wish you the best.

Brian P. Kelly, Publisher
Wilkes-Barre, Pennsylvania

# Table of Contents:

Chapter 1  The Best Student Debt Solution ........................................... 1

Chapter 2  No Problem Is Without a Solution ................................... 11

Chapter 3  Is the Student Loan Game Rigged? ................................. 23

Chapter 4:  Solving the Student Loan Crisis and the Housing Crisis .. 35

Chapter 5  What About a Progressive Loan Payback Schedule? ........ 43

Chapter 6  Forgive all Student Debt & Pay off the National Debt ..... 49

Chapter 7  Should We Fret About the Debt? ..................................... 61

Chapter 8  Congress Treats Student Borrowers Poorly ...................... 67

Chapter 9  Should I Go to College? .................................................... 73

Chapter 10  The Impact of Foreign Students ...................................... 87

Chapter 11  A Few Other Solid Solutions ........................................... 93

Chapter 12  Preventing New Massive Student Debt ......................... 103

Chapter 13  Reminder: Cost of an Undergraduate Degree ................ 111

Chapter 14  For-Profit Schools ......................................................... 117

Chapter 15  A Debt Plan for Student Debtors .................................. 127

# About the Author

Brian W. Kelly retired as an Assistant Professor in the Business Information Technology (BIT) program at Marywood University, where he also served as the IBM i and Midrange Systems Technical Advisor to the IT Faculty. Kelly designed, developed, and taught many college and professional courses. He continues as a contributing technical editor to a number of IT industry magazines, including "The Four Hundred" and "Four Hundred Guru," published by IT Jungle.

Kelly is a former IBM Senior Systems Engineer and IBM Mid Atlantic Area Specialist. His specialty was designing applications for customers as well as implementing advanced IBM operating systems and software facilities on their machines.

He has an active information technology consultancy. He is the author of 136 books and numerous technical articles. Kelly has been a frequent speaker at COMMON, IBM conferences, and other technical conferences.

Brian was a candidate for US Congress from Pennsylvania in 2010 and he brings a lot of experience to his writing endeavors.

Brian Kelly knows that the student debt crisis can be solved without bankrupting America.